Sociology on the Internet: A Student's Guide

Andrew T. Stull
California State University, Fullerton

Adapted by

Nijole V. Benokraitis
University of Baltimore

and

Andrius T. Benokraitis
Virginia Polytechnic Institute and State University

Prentice Hall, *Upper Saddle River, NJ 07458*

Editor: Nancy Roberts
Marketing Manager: Chaun Hightower

Copyright © 1997 by Prentice-Hall, Inc.
Simon & Schuster/A Viacom Company
Upper Saddle River, New Jersey 07458

Printed in the United States of America

ISBN 0-13-495649-4

TRADEMARK INFORMATION:
AIR Mosaic is a trademark of SPRY Incorporated;
America Online is a registered trademark of Quantum Computer Services Incorporated;
Cello is a trademark of Cornell Law School;
CompuServe is a trademark of CompuServe, Incorporated;
Delphi is a trademark of Delphi Internet Services Corporation;
Enhanced NCSA Mosaic is a trademark of Spyglass Incorporated;
InterAp is a trademark of California Software Incorporated;
Microsoft Windows and Internet Explorer are trademarks of Microsoft Corporation;
NCSA Mosaic is a trademark of the National Center for Supercomputing Applications;
NetCruiser is a trademark of Netcom On-Line Communications Services Incorporated;
Netscape is a registered trademark of Netscape Communications Corporation;
PageMill and SiteMill are registered trademarks of Adobe Corporation;
Prodigy is a registered trademark of Prodigy Systems Incorporated;
Web Explorer is a trademark of IBM Corporation;
WinTapestry is a trademark of Frontier Technologies Corporation;
WinWeb is a trademark of EINet Corporation.

The author and publisher of this manual have used their best efforts in preparing this book. The author and publisher make no warranty of any kind, expressed or implied, with regard to these programs or the documentation contained in this book. The author and publisher shall not be liable in any event for incidental or consequential damages in connection with, or arising out of, the furnishing, performance, or use of the programs described in this book.

Contents

Preface   *Change!*   vii

Introduction   *O' Brave New World:* Brief Internet History   1

Chapter 1   *The Mechanics:* Navigation Strategies   4

    1.1   What your mechanic never told you.   5
    1.2   Return to sender—address unknown.   9
    Activity: *365 Adventures Without Ever Leaving Home.*   13

Chapter 2   *Caught in the Net*   14

    2.1   Let your fingers do the walking.   14
    2.2   Sociology resources.   17
    Activity: *The Great Cyberspace Hunt.*   19

Chapter 3   *Doing Your Own Tune-up:* Advanced Techniques   21

    3.1   I prefer it *my* way!   22
    3.2   Do you get the news delivered?   26
    3.3   There's no place like home.   31
    Activity: *Make Yourself At Home*   38

Glossary   It's all Greek to me   39

Appendix

I   What's under the hood?
      (Basic Components)   44
II   Eyeglasses and spyglasses
      (List of Browsers)   47
III   A call to order
      (List of Service Providers)   49
IV   It's news to me
      (List of Sociology Newsgroups)   51
V   Stepping out
      (Homepage Template)   53

Acknowledgments

I'd like to thank my wife, Elizabeth, for the encouragement, the faith, and the unbelievable time she has spent editing this work. She has probably spent as many hours reviewing and providing invaluable suggestions for it as I have spent writing it. I must also thank my partner and mentor Steven Brunasso for his patience, friendship, and unbelievable clarity of vision for the Internet. I am grateful to the following people for providing many helpful comments and suggestions:

Susan Brawley, *University of Maine*
Ronald Edwards, *University of Florida*
Patrick A. Thorpe, *Grand Valley State University*
Robin Tyser, *University of Wisconsin—LaCrosse*
Roberta Williams, *University of Nevada, Las Vegas*

I am also grateful to Ray Mullaney, Editor in Chief of Engineering, Science, and Mathematics Development, who meticulously edited the final draft, and to Kelly McDonald, Executive Marketing Manager, for her insightful comments and guidance. Finally, I would like to thank Sheri Snavely, my editor at Prentice Hall, for listening to my rantings about the direction of education on the Internet, for the opportunity to write this manual, and for her support.

* *

We thank Elizabeth Kendall, Project Director at Prentice Hall, for her patience and support throughout this project. We are especially grateful to Vitalius Benokraitis for his intelligent suggestions, good humor, innumerable hours of assistance, and ensuring the technical accuracy of the material.

Nijole V. Benokraitis is Professor of Sociology at the University of Baltimore. Her son and slave, Andrius T. Benokraitis, is an undergraduate computer science major at Virginia Polytechnic Institute and State University.

Preface

Change! As I write this manual the time is 7:22 p.m., July 23, 1995. It might be a little odd that I should bother with such a seemingly insignificant statement but this brings me back to my first statement, "Change!" We live in a world that is in constant flux and has always been in such a state. It is a world louder, faster, and more complex than the one other generations have experienced. If you agree with me, you will recognize where we, as a techno-generation, are going and where our parents, as a paper-generation, are coming from. On the evening of this night, July 23rd, the Internet (a little more than 25 years old) and its most recent incarnation, the *World Wide Web* (about five years old), are changing at chaotic rates—revealing glimpses of our future. The information and resources that will be available to us tomorrow, July 24th, will have been amplified by this change and the world will be different.

I am writing this manual not to teach you all there is to know about the *World Wide Web* (*WWW* or simply called the *Web*), but rather to help you teach yourself. If I were to give you information without teaching you how to find it yourself, then you would be dependent on me and the bearer of old knowledge. If I and others are successful, your skills in 'surfing' the Internet will allow you to deal with the perpetual change. Eventually, we will laugh at ourselves as we watch later generations skillfully and artfully navigate this sea of information. If you don't believe me, tell a five-year-old that you need help operating the television remote. I suspect that they would think you silly.

By the end of the manual, you should be comfortable and resourceful in navigating the complexity of the Internet, from its back eddies to its thriving thoroughfares.

There are three chapters to this manual. In the Introduction, *O' Brave New World*, I will describe the origin and the innovations behind the Internet and in Chapter 1, *The Mechanics*, I will give you a run-through on the use of a *Web* browser and describe how you can find your way along the endless alcoves of the Internet. The boxed-in and end-of-chapter exercises will give you practice in using your browser and at the same time expose you to some of the wonderful places on the Internet.

In Chapter Two, *Caught In the Net*, you'll learn several strategies for information searching. The boxes and end-of-chapter exercises will reinforce your navigational skills and help you search for some of the great sociology resources available to you on the Internet.

In Chapter Three, *Doing Your Own Tune-up*, I will explain some of the fine tuning and customizing you can perform on your *Web* browser to make it more responsive to your needs. Additionally, I'll offer some of the essentials to move you from an observer to an *enthusiastic* participant. The boxed-in and end-of-chapter exercises will help you reach out and make contact with others on the Internet.

Introduction
O' Brave New World

This thing that we now call the Internet has been around for just over twenty-five years and has been growing and changing ever since it first started. The reasons for its creation and growth are quite interesting and helpful in understanding its nature, terminology, and the people who have adopted it as home.

The Internet has been likened to something alive because of the way it grows and changes. The best description of the Internet is that it is not just a network but a network of networks. In the late 50s and early 60s, scientists and engineers realized the importance of sharing and communicating through their computers. As things go, many different groups attempted to develop a network language and most were successful. The ironic thing was that now there were many different computer networks that still couldn't speak the same language. It was the Tower of Babel all over again.

The Internet was born as the solution to this problem. The U.S. government paid for the development of a common network language (called a protocol), which was eventually shared freely. With time, the many isolated networks from all over the world adopted this language (called TCP/IP). There is no central Internet agency and therefore the Internet is independent of governments and regulation. It grows and changes from the common need and commitment of the people that use it.

Admittedly this type of network system isn't the most graceful—but it works. If you saw a diagram of this great big computer network you might easily recognize it as a spider's web. On this web, information can easily travel between any two points along many different paths. This web is called the "Internet" and it was born in 1969. Although the Internet is still used very extensively for scientific purposes, it is growing for many other reasons. If you're taking a sociology course, for example, you can use the Internet to send electronic (e-mail) messages to your professor, author(s) of your textbooks, or to your classmates; to locate important or recently-published materials for a course project or paper; to access reviews of books that you might be using in

1

class or for outside readings; to get tips on improving your writing; to chat with students from other countries who are taking sociology courses; and to obtain information about graduate programs or job opportunities. Increasingly, moreover, professors are using the Internet to "connect" students in different states or colleges and universities. Both students and faculty can exchange ideas at any hour of the day or night, pursue discussions outside of class, and communicate instantaneously.

The Internet is going through many changes in the way information is provided. Although its initial purpose was to allow a distributed system for scientific exchange and research, it gradually took on the role of a digital post office (electronic mail and file transfer). As technology changed, the transfer speed and the way we viewed the information changed. Earlier work on the Internet relied on a "command-line interface," where a user simply typed commands from a keyboard and waited for the response. DOS-controlled computers are an example of this. Recent advancements have brought us the graphical user interfaces (GUI). Macintosh and Microsoft Windows are classic examples of systems that use a GUI. These GUIs rely on icons and images to symbolize activities and commands. Actions are initiated with a mouse click instead of a typed command. One of the first commonly used GUIs for the Internet was *Gopher*, developed at the University of Minnesota in 1991 and named after its mascot, the gopher.

Gopher is a visual tool for the Internet, where information is presented as a hierarchical listing of directories and files. The users jump from general directories at higher levels to more specific directories at lower levels until they find what they want. Beyond searching for information on a single computer, *Gopher* allows the users to quickly and transparently jump from one computer to another. This method of interaction no longer requires the users to log-on to each computer independently but rather allows them to wander or <u>browse</u> (the *Gopher* people call this process "burrowing") at will among the vast stores of information on the world's computers. Once the information is found, it can easily be downloaded to the user's computer. By simplifying the access and use of the Internet, the number of users and businesses has increased at astronomical rates. Amazing if you think about it! You could be on your computer in Toledo, Ohio, jumping from one screen to another and suddenly find yourself in London, Mexico City, or Tokyo. Wham! And no airline tickets!

The next major tool for the Internet followed in 1991 with the creation of the *World Wide Web* information format, conceived and initiated at CERN in Switzerland. Although *Gopher*, as an initial attempt at navigating the Internet, was a good GUI, it lacked visual appeal.

Information on the *Web* is posted as a "page" and it may contain text, images, sounds, and movies. The organization of a page is much like any printed page in a book. There are the visual improvements but the major innovation is the use of *hypertext*. Hypertext, more specifically hypermedia, is the use of words *and* images as links or connecting points to different text, images, sounds, or movies on other computers throughout the world.

After the introduction of the *Web*, there was a dilemma: a great place to go but no easy way to get there. Kind of like the moon in the 60's. The one thing still lacking was a convenient program that would allow users to access the *Web* easily. This program, *Mosaic*, appeared in 1993 from the National Center for Supercomputing Applications (NCSA). Not only did *Mosaic* allow for the browsing of *Web* pages, but it added the ability to use other Internet resources such as e-mail, *Gopher*, and FTP. With the release of this browser, the *Web* has been growing faster than the speed of light. In 1991, there were around 700,000 Internet users. After *Mosaic* in 1993, the number increased to around 1.7 million. In July of 1994, the estimate was more than 3.2 million. In April 1996 there were an estimated 20 million Internet users, and the number of users was growing by 160,000 a month (no joke!). This phenomenal growth is attributed to the release of *Mosaic* and sister browsers like *Netscape*. Today the Internet is changing at staggering rates and becoming more readily available to the average person.

Chapter 1
The Mechanics

READY. SET. GO!—Do you remember hearing those words when you were a kid? I used to run foot races with my friends when I was young. The kid that yelled for the start would always jump the line before he called GO. I'd be slow off of the line in some races, fast in others, and occasionally I'd even win. But at the end of the race, it didn't matter because we'd all be happy and we'd do it again—possibly to a different finish.

In the real world, not everyone starts at the same time, but that does NOT determine the finish. In a similar way, many of you have had a lot of experience with computers, while others have none at all. To begin this chapter you should have your computer set up and operational, including the necessary software and an Internet connection. For those of you who are new to this race, fear not. I have included several resources in the *appendices* at the back of this guide to help you get started. These resources include a description of the necessary equipment (*Appendix I*), a list of the leading software (*Appendix II*), and a list of companies that would be glad to help you connect to the Internet for a small fee (*Appendix III*). After you read the appendices, you'll have an equal chance at the starting line.

Before you contact a commercial company, however, find out what your college/university offers. Many institutions have developed publications to help students get a "quick start" on the Internet. These guides probably also include advice on how to purchase, install, and connect to your college/university computer system from your home. If you run into problems getting everything to work, ask one of your friendly computer experts for help.

There are a staggering number of computers, software, and connections that you can use to get onto the Internet. This manual includes general features common to some different computers and software packages that you may be using. In certain situations, I made a personal choice so that this manual didn't become too generic or void of personality. Most notably, I have illustrated this manual using examples from the *Netscape* 2.0 software on a Macintosh. *Netscape* is a very good browser and *free* to students, educators, and schools.

Section 1.1
What your mechanic never told you.

The software that you'll use to access the Net is commonly called a *client* or a *Web browser*. It functions on an information exchange model called a *Client-Server model* (Figure 1). In this way, a client (your *Web* browser software) will communicate with a *server* (other *Web* server software) on the Internet to exchange information. When referring to the *Web*, the information that your browser receives from the server is called a *page*.

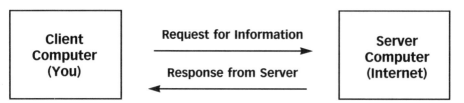

| Client Computer (You) | Request for Information →
← Response from Server | Server Computer (Internet) |

Figure 1. The Client requests information from the server. The requested information is displayed on the client computer.

So, what really appears on these *Web* pages? The best way is to see for yourself. If you can, sit down in front of a computer, start your browser software, and connect to the Internet. Your browser is probably already set to start at a specific page. This start page is often referred to as a *homepage*. *Web* pages usually include both text and images. Some will also use sounds and videos. The use of different information types is called multimedia. When you choose a page it will be sent to your computer. After the requested information has been sent by the server, your computer will display it for you. As a basic rule, anything that can be saved or recorded onto a computer can be provided and distributed on the Internet through a *Web* page.

GoTo

Because sometimes it is better to begin by running before you know how to walk, I've put this section first. Since the Internet is so vast, you may initially feel intimidated. Finding your way through the Internet and the *Web* is really no harder then finding your way to a friend's house. Suppose that your friends are having a party at their new house and supplying all the entertainment and food. You're familiar with their town, so you need only their address to get to the party. Navigating the Internet with a *Web* browser is even easier. If you want to go someplace on the *Web*, all you do is type the address into the browser and connect to the desired page. No map required.

Information on the Internet has an address just as your friends do. Most browsers allow you the option of typing in an address and going directly to that document. With *Netscape*, there are two easy ways to do this. The easiest way is to use the *Open* toolbar button. A small window will appear and offer you the opportunity to type in the address of the desired document. A second method, and also one employed by other browsers, is to modify the browser so that Internet addresses are viewable.

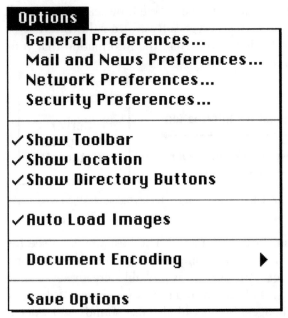

Figure 2. Within *Netscape*, some of the selections under the *Options* menu act as toggle buttons. They can be alternately turned on (with a check mark) or off (without a check mark) by clicking the mouse while the option is highlighted (or selected). Other options display submenus allow further customization.

With *Netscape,* you can open this window by selecting *Show Location* from the *Options* menu (Figure 2). The address window (see Figure 3) will appear immediately below the toolbar buttons. Just type in the requested addresses and press the return button on your keyboard.

Figure 3. With the *Show Location* option selected in the *Option* menu the *Goto* window will appear on your browser just below the toolbar.

Navigation

You don't always have to know the address of a page to view it. The wonderful thing about the *Web* is that you can access (navigate) pages through the use of *hyperlinks*. Hyperlinks are a functional part of moving around the *Web*. You will notice these hyperlinks as colored (non-black) words on the page. Images, graphs, or maps may also be hyperlinks. Select or click on the desired hyperlink for a new page of information. Some *Web* authors write their pages so that their hyperlinks are hidden from you. If you are new, just click on everything. You can't break it.

With recent innovations in writing *Web* pages, other interactions are possible. Clickable images or maps are becoming a prominent way of interacting with *Web* pages. With a clickable image, you have the option to select/click a section on the image, which functions as a hyperlink. This is different from the normal image link because the author of a *Web* page can connect one image to many different places. An example might be a map of the United States (or other countries). The creator of such a document might place a hyperlink for graphs showing poverty rates, homicide rates, divorce rates and so on. Clicking on each state (or country in Europe) could take you to different pages of information.

Here are three addresses that use clickable maps. They are also great places to find sociological information.

http://www.uib.no/nsd/diverse/utenland.htm
http://www.epa.gov/oar/
http://www.census.gov/ces/themapit/

Not all browsers support clickable maps but most good *Web* authors will still provide the same choices using conventional hyperlinks.

Hyperlinks are great for navigating the Internet. However, there are many documents that don't incorporate hyperlinks. If you end up on one of these pages, you'll need another method of navigation or you'll be in trouble. This is very similar to driving though a neighborhood, turning the corner onto a dead end and realizing you don't have a reverse gear. The solution, of course, is to *have* a reverse gear. All good browsers incorporate basic features, such as *Back* and *Forward*, to allow the user to hop between recently viewed pages.

Although I'm using the *Netscape* browser to illustrate points for the manual, you'll find that most browsers differ in the appearance only to the degree that their toolbar buttons for basic navigation are in different order (something you can handle). Figure 4 illustrates the basic orientation of the navigation buttons for *Netscape* 2.0.

Figure 4. The *Netscape Navigator* 2.0 *Web* browser offers a wide selection of basic navigation and control buttons in the toolbar. Although this is a representation of the control strip from the Macintosh version, the *Windows* version is identical in function and appearance. The toolbars from other browsers offer similar functions.

One of the most useful features that you'll use is the *Home* button. This feature allows you to jump back to your homepage. We'll discuss how to choose and set your homepage later in the manual. Two additional buttons common to most browsers are the *Reload* and *Stop* buttons. *Netscape* also includes many other features within its toolbar to give you flexibility in navigating the Internet, but they are self-explanatory and may differ from some of the options provided by other browser programs.

Don't wait until the last minute. Use one of the addresses we gave you and experiment with the buttons on your browsers. If you want something different, try the following addresses.

http://www.yahoo.com/index.html
http://lycos.cs.cmu.edu
http://www.asanet.org/

Yahoo! and *Lycos* are information directories. You can search using any sociological categories or topics. The last address is for the American Sociological Association. Remember you won't break anything and if you get lost, you can always begin again.

Up to now, everything on a *Web* page has been described as a point, click, and jump. A new feature called *Forms* has added an entirely new dimension for both the user and the creator of *Web* pages. On some *Web* pages, you will find a section where you may be asked to give information by typing from the keyboard. This information might be a survey, an answer to a question, or your request to a *Web* server. In sociology, forms may be used for information retrieval. As the box below shows, you can get valuable information from organizations, government agencies, and educational institutions.

Experiment with the following links which involve forms. If you got this far, then you are well off the start line. Not all browsers support forms so you will need to determine if yours does.

http://www.census.gov/cdrom/lookup/
http://www.lib.virginia.edu/socsci/world/world.country.html
http://www.votelink.com/

Section 1.2
Return to sender—address unknown

The addresses that you've been using on the *Web* are called Universal Resource Locators, or URLs for short. Each URL (pronounced "earl") has a couple of basic parts just like a residential address. Look at some of the URLs (now you know what they are called) that you've used already. Do you notice any common features or similarities between them?

Here is yet another example of a typical URL and a pretty useful site in itself. There are three basic components to a URL. Compare this with the others I've given to you.

http://www.charm.net/CWSApps/cwsa.html

Here are the three components:

protocol	http://
server	www.charm.net
path	/CWSApps/cwsa.html

Be careful. Even one incorrect character will prevent the browser from finding the correct site.

It may seem confusing at first, but think of it as nothing more than a postal address squished together without any spaces. The protocol of the URL denotes how the information is stored. In the exercise above, "HTTP" refers to the protocol or language for which all *Web* servers speak. The colon and slashes are used to separate it from the name of the server. They are not always present with every type of URL. The path describes the location of the *Web* page on the server.

Up until this point, we have only been discussing browsers as a way of navigating through information using hyperlinks. However, browsers also have the power to link to other, much older, formats of information. Try the following URLs to notice how the information differs.

ftp://oak.oakland.edu/pub3
gopher://gopher.micro.umn.edu:70/1

The HTTP, FTP, and Gopher are not the only resources, but they are the three you're most likely to encounter. Have you ever encountered the following Internet protocols?

telnet://
wais://
news:

9

The last part of the server name defines the domain to which the server belongs. A domain is just a fancy name for a functional network group. The most common domain that you'll see is the .edu domain that encompasses educational institutions.

Some of the other domains you are likely to encounter are *com*, *gov*, *mil*, *net*, and *org*. Here are some examples that you might be interested in. Com stands for "commercial." Can you determine what the other domains represent?

http://www.toyota.com	**Not Just About Cars**
http://www.whitehouse.gov/	**The White House**
http://www.dtic.dla.mil/defenselink/	**Armed Forces Defense Link**
http://plaza.interport.net/listenup/	**Listen Up!**
http://envirolink.org/	**Envirolink Online**

In your travels, you will eventually jump to a server that is outside your country. Much, but not all, of the information on these servers is in English (so unless you are paying attention you might never know your foreign whereabouts). URLs of foreign servers have an additional section at the end of the server's name. It is a two letter code that denotes the country. Here are just a few examples but I trust that you can find more.

- .au   Australia
- .ca   Canada
- .ch   Switzerland
- .lt   Lithuania
- .nl   Netherlands
- .pe   Peru
- .uk   United Kingdom

Bookmarks

Now that you've found so many *really* interesting pages, how do you find them again a day or a week from now? This is where bookmarks come in. You place a bookmark on the page to which you wish to return. Just to get your collection started, try this address: **http://www.hotwired.com**. It's the on-line version of *Wired Magazine* and a pretty interesting place. If you like their page, you can save a bookmark by selecting *Add Bookmark* from the *Bookmarks* menu on your browser (Figure 5). Some browsers may be different. *Mosaic* uses the term *Hotlist* instead of *Bookmark*, but the same general idea applies. Now, if you use your mouse to go back to the *Bookmarks* menu, you'll see that *Hotwired* is just a jump away. You don't have to memorize the URL and you don't have to haphazardly jump around until you find it again.

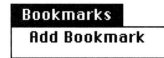

Figure 5. After you've added bookmarks to your browser, they will appear in a list under the *Bookmarks . . .* menu on the menubar. Once you've selected a list of bookmarks, you may use the *View Bookmarks . . .* to arrange and organize them into categories.

Ack! What happens when you've stored too many bookmarks and you can't find anything anymore? In *Netscape 2.0*, there is a new interactive bookmarking tool, which allows you to create groups of folders to organize URLs by topic and even insert seperators for easy visibility. Just go into the *Bookmarks* menu (see Figure 6), create a folder, and drag your bookmark into the newly-created folder.

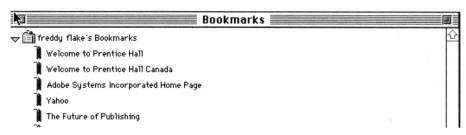

Figure 6. To start arranging your bookmarks into categories click on the *Windows* menu bar then the *Bookmarks . . .* option. A window will appear to allow you to organize your bookmarks.

It is possible to export your bookmarks as a group so that you can give them to others. It's similar to trading baseball cards or recipes. I won't go into the procedures here, but as with life, it's yours, use it wisely, learn, and have fun.

Travel History

If you've been working along with your manual and your browser at the same time, you've probably been to many places on the *Web*. Obviously, if you want to move back and forth between your selections you are probably using the *Forward* and *Back* buttons on the browser's toolbar. But what do you do if you want to go back to someplace you've visited fifteen jumps ago? Do you press the *Back* button fifteen times? Well, if you choose to do it that way, *fine*, but it is a little slow. There is a great feature that allows you to jump rapidly to any of the places you've visited along your path of travel. If you are using the *Netscape* browser then click on the *GO* menu option and you'll see a list of all of the places you've visited on your journey. Other browsers have similar features. The simple point is that without using the *Back* button fifteen times, you can select from a list of recently-viewed pages.

Now that you've got the hang of it, give the following URLs a try.

http://www.starwave.com/
Link to TicketMaster, ESPN SportsZone, and More
http://www.pointcom.com/
Surf the Best Web Sites
http://www.pctravel.com/
Airline Ticketing Online
http://www.cdnow.com/
CDNow Online Music Shopping
http://ucsu.colorado.edu/~cullison/newwave/songs.html
Early 80's Song of the Week
http://www.new3.com/riddle/
Brain Teasers
http://www.pigweb.com/
Digital Art
http://www.gildamarx.com/
Women's Exercise Clothes (Virtual Reality with QuickTime)
http://www.caranddriver.com/
Car and Driver Online
http://www.usps.gov/
Zip Codes
http://www.xmission.com/~mgm/quotes
Quotations Page
http://postcards.www.media.mit.edu/postcards/
Electronic Postcards
http://www.culturefinder.com/
Performing Arts, People, and Related News
http://www.misty.com/laughweb/
Take a Humor Break
http://www.parentsplace.com/
Online Parenting
http://www.uc.edu/~taylorrm/index.html
Historical Myths and Conspiracies
http://wheel.ucdavis.edu/~btcarrol/skeptic/dictcont.html
The Skeptic's Dictionary

When you find something that you think is fun and interesting, save it or give it to a friend.

Activity
365 Adventures Without Ever Leaving Home

I hope that you haven't waited until this point to travel the *Web*. But if you have, this exercise will get you up to speed. You'll have plenty of opportunity to experience some of the great places that are at your disposal on the Internet. The only thing that you'll need is the knowledge of reading URLs and saving bookmarks.

If you really like the unpredictable nature of randomly jumping around the Internet you might want to visit these random jump *Web* pages. You will be riding a roulette wheel to resources on the Internet. This allows you to jump to a random document potentially anywhere in the world. With each *Web* document, check the URL.

http://www.uroulette.com:8000/
Uroulette Homepage

http://www.netcreations.com/coolroulette/
Cool Roulette

http://cs.utexas.edu/users/usamaw/links.html
URL Randomizer

This exercise is really a free ride. You will experience many different places and discover some that have value to you. If you find something that you like, set a bookmark or record the URL so that you can return.

1. Compile a list of the different countries you visit. You have been given a basic set of country domain codes. How many more can you find?
2. How many foreign languages can you find? English is probably the most common but definitely not the only one you'll encounter.

Netscape and many other browsers allow you to organize bookmarks into categories. It is easy to find the information in the user manual. Try categories like: *Fun and Games, Magazines, News and Weather, Outdoors,* and *Sociology*. Under each of these major categories you can create subcategories. Using sociology as an example, I might have subcategories like: *Census Data, Women's Studies, Newsgroups,* etc . . .

3. Organize your bookmarks into categories so that they are easy to use. Use the categories that I've described above or make your own.

Chapter 2
Caught In The Net

In Chapter 1 you learned what the Internet is, how to use a browser, and what resources are available to you through the *Web*. If you've done your homework, you'll also realize that you have no chance of memorizing the content or location of everything at your disposal. This leads us into our next major point. Since there is little hope of ever memorizing all of that information, then your best bet is to learn how to *find* information when you need it. If you remember, the first chapter really covered the technique of browsing, which is just the haphazard wandering from one place to another. Here, you will learn to search actively for specific information.

Section 2.1
Let your fingers do the walking.

Although there is plenty of valuable information on the Internet, it is not always simple to find it. The tools that I'll describe here are free and easy to use; but you should remember that searching for information on the Internet or elsewhere is a skill that needs to be practiced.

The Internet is so flexible and diverse that even if there is something that isn't on the net, you can always add your ideas to it, and then add your URL to the *Web* so that others can see your work. Later we will explain how to write basic *Web* pages, but for now here are some of the more popular searching tools on the *World Wide Web* today.

Search Engines and Directories

A search engine is nothing more than a program that runs a search for you while you're waiting for the results. There are many search engines on the *Web* and other places like *Gopher*. *Archie*, *Veronica*, and *Jughead* are search

14

engines that are available to search different aspects of the Internet like *Gopher* and FTP. We won't cover them here, but as you build your experience and confidence, you should give them a try. Some of the *Web* search engines are commercial and they may charge you a fee to run a search. Just as anything that proves itself to be in demand, the *Web* is turning commercial and you will notice many places will begin as a free service and eventually ask you to pay a fee. Don't worry; there are plenty of free search engines and many more popping up all the time.

A search engine that some people use frequently is called *WebCrawler* (**http://www.Webcrawler.com/**). It's very simple to operate but, as with any search tool, it takes practice and patience to master. Take time now to connect to *WebCrawler*, and we'll take it for a test run. When you first see the opening page, you'll notice that it is very simple. Fear not; behind this page is a very good resource. Reading the instructions on the page will tell you most everything you need to know. Enter a word into the white entry box and press the submit button, *WebCrawler* will refer back to its database of information and return a page of hyperlinked resources containing the word you entered. When the query results come back to you, notice that they are hyperlinks to somewhere out on the *Web*.

Yahoo! (**http://www.yahoo.com**) is a great searching tool. It is only one of many directories that is available on the Internet but it is the best for general topics. Maneuvering through *Yahoo!* is a breeze if you want to find URLs by topic. As you become more experienced and travel the Web you'll discover more. As we describe this tool, follow along and experiment with it.

Yahoo! is a listing of information by category—kind of like a card catalog. At the top of the listing, there are several very general categories, but as you move deeper into the directory you'll notice that the categories become more specific. To find information, you simply choose the most appropriate category at the top level and continue through each successive level until you find what you're looking for or until you realize you're in the wrong place. Don't worry, it's not unusual to get lost. Just begin again and try different categories.

As an example, suppose you were studying a chapter on marriage and the family and you wanted to learn more. Within *Yahoo!*, notice that two of the top level categories are Society and Culture and Social Science. Since the Social Science category includes Sociology, it would seem to be the most appropriate place to find the information so give it a try. After accessing the Social Science category, you'll notice that it gives a list of many different types of social science. So, what is your next choice? My choice is Sociology because I'm in a Sociology course, but Psychology, Social Work and Genealogy are also possibilities. Because *Yahoo!* cross references among the categories, you'll find that several related categories will lead you to your desired page.

Much of your success in finding information with this type of tool requires a little imagination. Often, it is possible to find material on a topic in a category that you may not consider initially. Again, let's take the example of marriage and the family. Are you especially interested in racial/ethnic families? If so, you might search under such Social Science subcategories as African-American Studies, Asian-American Studies, or Institutes.

Prepare yourself for a search *before* you jump into one. In the long run it will save you both time and frustration. Don't be afraid to try some unusual approaches in your search strategy. Think of all the associations that your query may have and give them each a try. You never know when it will turn up a gold mine.

Other Search Engines

Although our list is far from comprehensive, several other commonly-used search engines include *Lycos*, *Excite!*, and *Alta Vista*. Search engines work in many different ways—some search titles or headers of documents, others search the documents themselves, and still others search other directories. Explore as many as possible before deciding which work best for you.

Lycos (http://lycos.cs.cmu.edu/) is one of the largest search engines today with more than 3 million URLs. *Lycos* is a comprehensive catalog of the Internet and finds what you need in seconds, including text, graphics, sounds, and videos. Besides its ability to find even complex topics and keywords, *Lycos* provides a directory of the most popular sites as well as critical reviews of the *Web's* top sites.

Excite! (http://www.excite.com/) is one of the newest searching engines. It is very versatile because it tracks down information by searching for concepts, not just keywords. Suppose, for example, that you're interested in material on age discrimination. *Excite!* can find such information even though the source describes the phenomenon (such as bias against older people) without ever using the phrase "age discrimination." It also provides you with a percentage of how close it "thinks" it came to providing pertinent information on your concept(s). *Excite!* also has such capabilities as finding a specific news article from newsgroups by a text search.

Alta Vista (http://www.altavista.digital.com) offers general and detailed searches through what the Digital Equipment Corporation claims is the largest *Web* index. According to *Alta Vista*, the user has access to nearly 11 billion words found in nearly 22 million *Web* pages. In addition, you can access a full-text index of more than 13,000 newsgroups.

InfoSeek Guide (http://guide.infoseek.com) is a free search/browse service, which returns both search hits and a list of topics related to your search. With each search, you get the most relevant matches, related topics to explore, and current news and views from popular magazines, TV networks, and online experts. *InfoSeek Guide* also helps you find e-mail addresses, stock quotes, company profiles, and other materials.

Now that you have a grasp of a few of the different search engines used today, you can find even more on the Internet. For example, **SEARCH.COM** (http://www.search.com/) helps you use over 250 search engines, including those we already described. It also provides hundreds of specialized databases.

Section 2.2
Sociology resources.

The Internet is a booming and rapidly-developing creature. The only way to find out which search engines give you the best results is to try them. If you've tried searching under such topics as marriage, family, or age discrimination that we discussed earlier, you probably got some results that didn't seem to apply to your research topic. Did you find, for example, that some of your hits included announcements of past or future professional family therapy conferences? If you said yes, then you've noticed one of the downfalls of search engines. They are very fast and very dumb. They don't think. That is *your* job. Despite some misses, however, you'll find that search engines are very powerful tools and will save you time in the long run.

Increasingly, moreover, there is a growing list of specific URLs that can help you focus your research and prepare your search strategies. Some of these sites are provided below.

Here are a few sociology and social science links that should ignite your sociological imagination. Two cautions are in order, however. First, don't be discouraged if your first try produces a message like "Unable to connect to remote host." The rule of thumb is to try the same site three times in a row before proceeding to another URL. Second, be careful not to use the number 1 when you need the letter l (L). Remember that if you mistype one character, the address won't work. Note, finally, that the tilde (~) designates a site maintained by a person, rather than an organization or some other "non-person." Have fun!

Sociology Internet Resources*
http://www.umsl.edu/~sociolog/resource.htm

Social Sciences WWW Resources
**http://coombs.anu.edu.au/WWWVLPages/SocialPages/
  SocSci-1.html**
**http://coombs.anu.edu.au/WWWVLPages/SocialPages/
  SocSci-2.html**

The American Sociological Association
http://www.asanet.org/

Sociology Server
http://www.webcom.com/dread/socio.html

Sociological Methodology
http://weber.u.washington.edu/~socmeth2/

Women's Studies and Other Women's Resources
**http://inform.umd.edu:86/Educational_Resources/
  AcademicResourcesByTopic/WomensStudies/**
http://sunsite.unc.edu/cheryb/women/wresources.html

Race and Ethnicity Resources
http://pwa.acusd.edu/~hinman/race.html
http://pantheon.cis.yale.edu/~davidp/race.html

*This site includes such resources as centers of research, organizations, electronic journals and newsletters, archives, and provides instructions for subscribing to more than 50 sociology discussion groups in the United States, Canada, and Europe. The discussion group topics include racial and ethnic relations, popular culture, computer use, research methodology, family, sexual orientation, graduate students, sports, and women's studies.

Activity
The Great Cyberspace Hunt.

Here's what you've all been waiting for! I've been keeping my ear close to the ground listening for information on sociology in the popular press and media. The first list is a set of some commonly-heard sociological terms. See what you can find on these topics. Try to find the information in the least number of jumps possible. How have each of these terms enhanced our understanding of our society?

- Latchkey Children
- Zero Population Growth
- Sexual Harassment
- Deadbeat Dads
- Chain Migration
- Affirmative Action
- Fetal Alcohol Syndrome
- Underemployment
- Open Adoption
- Date Rape

Understanding sociology often means learning about the women and men who have made significant contributions in both theory and methodology. Below is a short list of some pioneering social thinkers from the nineteenth and twentieth centuries. Some of them will be very easy to track down while others will not. We hope you'll find both their perspectives and their lives interesting.

Your assignment is to put together a brief history of some of the social scientists listed below and their important contributions. If you want more of a challenge, suggest four substitutions and explain the reasons for your choices.

- Howard S. Becker
- Jessie Bernard
- Ruth Benedict
- Auguste Comte
- Alexis de Tocqueville
- W.E. B. Du Bois
- Emile Durkheim
- Erving Goffman
- Rose Hum Lee
- Audre Lorde
- Karl Marx

- George Herbert Mead
- Margaret Mead
- Robert K. Merton
- C. Wright Mills
- Talcott Parsons
- Ronald Takaki
- Max Weber

Remember to use all of the resources at your disposal that we described throughout this chapter. Check the obscure as well as the popular resources. If you'd like to see a lighter side during your search, access the Sociology Server URL provided on the previous page and click on "Goodman's Sociology for Very Short Attention Spans." In addition, you might read ahead to Chapter 3 and use e-mail and newsgroup resources if they are helpful.

Chapter 3
Doing Your Own Tune-up

I'm sure that by now you understand the direction of this manual. In Chapter 1 you were introduced to the depth and breadth of the *Web*. Through several exercises I helped you to wander and drift with the hope that you'd understand the potential of the resource you have at your disposal. Some may say that this was like Moses in the desert but I hope that it was more like a kid in a candy store. In Chapter 2, I introduced you to the skills you'd need to walk your own path. Due to the vastness of the *Web*, effective searching is vital if you wish to tame the *Web* for purposeful study. This last chapter will cover some of the advanced techniques to help you make your *Web* experience more enjoyable and profitable.

I've illustrated this manual with *Netscape Navigator 2.0* because I feel that it is the best browser on the market independent of the fact that it is free to education. Even though I've chosen *Netscape*, I encourage you to make up your own mind. You may find that another is more appropriate for you. Whatever you choose, the following descriptions and techniques should still help. Remember, the *Web* adventure is not in *what* you use, but *how* you use it.

So that you have something for comparison, here are the homepages for the three most prominent *Web* browsers, *Microsoft Internet Explorer*, *Mosaic* and *Netscape*. Within these pages you will also find the manuals for each program.

http://www.microsoft.com/ie/iedl.htm
**http://www.ncsa.uiuc.edu/SDG/Software/Mosaic/NCSAMosaic
Home.html**
http://home.netscape.com/

Section 3.1
I prefer it *my* way!

Know your options and you'll save both time and money. On the Internet, and as a matter of fact, in life, "Time is money." According to Einstein, "Time is relative"; so I guess you could also say—"Time is relative to the amount of money you have." I wonder if Einstein thought of this? No, I'm not rambling. Here is where I get to the point. If you are like me, you don't have much money, and time is very relative if you have to use a modem and a service provider to surf. If you know what your browser can and cannot do, and if you configure the options for your browser so that it is most efficient for you, you will save oodles of time. With *Netscape*, under the *Options* menu (Figure 7) you are allowed several choices to customize the appearance and function of your browser. I'll say it again, don't wait for me. Try these techniques as you go along and jump around to the information that is important to you.

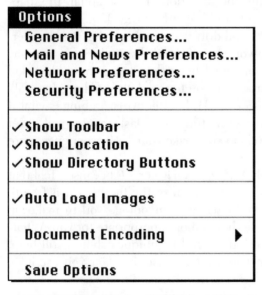

Figure 7. Many of the general options are listed in the *Options* menu on *Netscape*, but if you wish to do a more detailed configuration, you can find more options under the various *Preferences* . . . submenus.

I described some of these options previously, and some of you may have already experimented with the others but here is an explanation for the rest of you. Notice that there is a check mark by some of the options. Look at *Auto Load Images* as an example. When the check is present, images will be automatically loaded. If you select this option again, the check mark disappears and subsequently, pages will load the text without the time-consuming images. Give it a try. If you're trying to connect to the Internet through a modem, as I frequently do, you've probably noticed that some of those images, sounds, and videos take a long time to download to your computer. This, in itself, isn't a big deal until you consider that some pages are crammed with images and downloading them requires a lot of time. This really digs into your wallet if you pay an hourly connection rate to your service provider. What I do to save some money and frustration is to turn off the automatic image load on my browser until I get to a place of interest. In a similar fashion, the other options from this pull-down menu work much the same.

> The following is the URL for the *Netscape* handbook. You should refer to it whenever my ramblings stop making sense to you. You will also find other resources that will help you so don't hesitate to give it a look.
>
> ### http://home.netscape.com/eng/mozilla/2.0/handbook/

If this isn't enough control for you, there are other changes you can make. Notice the various *Preferences . . .* submenus under *Options* (Figure 7). When you select one of these, you will be presented with a series of dialog windows, where you can choose even more customizing options. If you don't like the way the font, color, or style of the text that appears on your browser, you can change them within this dialog window. Browsers typically provide you with many features to allow you to change the visual appearance of the information on the viewed page.

After opening the *General Preferences . . .* dialog window, a window containing several "folders" of options will appear for you to select. Each of these options will take you to a different preference window. Figure 8 shows the folders you may select when customizing your browser. This dialog window usually opens to the category you were last modifying, so don't be disoriented when it looks different each time.

| Appearance | Colors | Fonts | Helpers | Images | Applications | Languages |

Toolbars
Show Toolbar as: ○ Pictures   ○ Text   ● Pictures and Text

Startup
On Startup Launch: ● Netscape Browser   ○ Netscape Mail   ○ Netscape News

Browser starts with:
   ○ Blank Page
   ● Home Page Location: http://home.netscape.com/

Link Styles
Links are: ☒ Underlined
Followed Links Expire: ○ Never   ● After 30 days   [Now]

Figure 8.   There are many choices available to you from within the *General Preferences* menu.

One of the first preferences that you might want to modify is the location of your default homepage. When you first start your browser, it looks for a page from which to start. A homepage is like "home base" in a game of hopscotch. It is the place you begin hopping from square to square. If you're working with a browser that hasn't been customized before, it probably has the homepage set to the company that made it. If you're working on one of your school's computers, then the homepage may already be set to the school's page. If neither is the case, then within the *Appearance* preference folder (Figure 9) you have the option to designate a homepage. By now you've probably found something on the *Web* that you are willing to call home. Enter the URL as illustrated below and every time you start your browser or select home from the toolbar you'll end up at this URL. Later in this chapter we'll discuss how you can make and display your own homepage. Stay tuned. Notice that you also have the option of modifying the appearance of your toolbar.

```
,Toolbars ............................................................................................
 Show Toolbar as :     ○ Pictures    ◉ Text    ○ Pictures and Text

,Startup ...............................................................................................
 On Startup Launch :  ◉ Netscape Browser  ○ Netscape Mail  ○ Netscape News

 Browser starts with :
        ○ Blank Page
        ◉ Home Page Location :  [http://web.server.url/home_page.html]
```

Figure 9. Your browser is easily customized to display your toolbar and homepage preferences.

On the *Appearance* preference folder you also have the option of customizing the appearance of your hyperlinks. Hopefully, you've noticed that hyperlinks are normally blue (this is if you or someone else hasn't changed the default color). Once you've accessed them, they change to purple. It lets you know that you've already been down that link and that therefore you should select a different path. You can set the length of time for a hyperlink before it changes back to the default color. As illustrated in Figure 10, I have my link expiration set to one day. Notice that you can have the browser underline the hyperlinks or leave them plain.

```
,Link Styles .........................................................................................
            Links are :   ☒ Underlined
  Followed Links Expire :  ○ Never  ◉ After [1] days  [ Now ]
```

Figure 10. The appearance of hyperlinks should be set to match the degree to which you travel the Internet. If you travel frequently, you may find that your hyperlinks will always disappear and is therefore set too high. If you travel infrequently, you may find it is best never to expire a traveled link.

If you select the *Fonts* preference folder you will see a dialog window (Figure 11) that will allow you to modify the font style and size of the text as displayed by your browser. If you typically have a difficult time reading small text from a computer screen, then you may want to increase the size or style of the font.

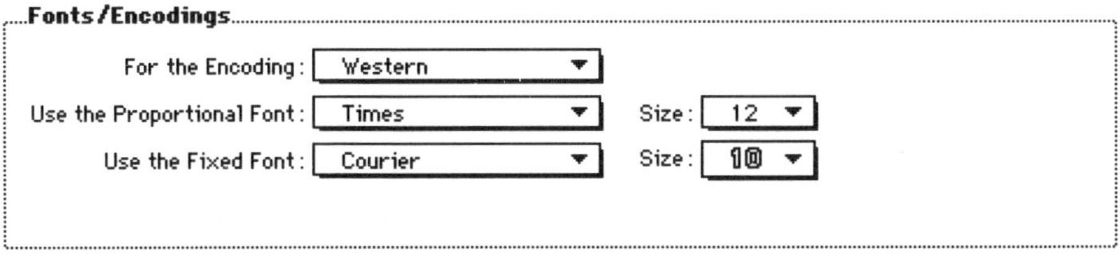

Figure 11. Selecting a font of appropriate style and size will help you prevent eye strain and muscle fatigue from leaning over your computer to read.

As with fonts, the default text, hyperlink, and background colors can be modified on your browser to meet your individual preferences (use the *Colors* folder—Figure 12). My suggestion is to set the colors so that you maximize the contrast between the components.

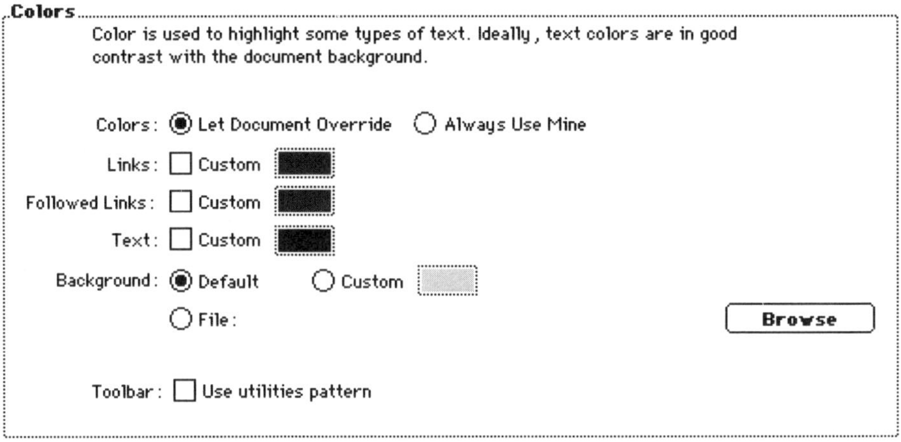

Figure 12. Customizing the colors of the components on your browser will help you quickly identify hyperlinks and navigational paths as you travel.

I have not covered all of the options available to you for customizing your browser. An extensive explanation is available to you through the *Netscape* homepage. If you are using another browser, you will find that it has similar options, and on occasion some browsers may give you more power to control

25

your browser's appearance. Again, it doesn't matter which browser *you* choose to use, just make sure it works for all the pages you access. Not all browsers work the same. Some may show tables differently than others, and some authors of *Web* pages even code for a specific browser because of its particular capabilities.

Section 3.2
Do you get the news delivered?

Learning is a give-and-take activity. It is an interchange of ideas. Effective learning involves communication between all those involved—instructors and students. This means that students need to learn how to communicate among themselves. Within any learning environment, people may bring a different and unique perspective. With the interchange of ideas, experiences, and understandings shared by each person, the whole community benefits. This brings me to my next point. *Netscape* and many other browsers have incorporated the ability to allow you to communicate through e-mail, newsgroups, and on-line interest groups.

E-mail

As we've discussed earlier, e-mail is the electronic exchange of mail among people. This exchange is from one person to another person. E-mail follows a similar Client-Server model as do *Web* browsers and *Web* servers. Your client software asks a server computer for new items of mail addressed to you. Your mail server is operated and maintained by the administrator of your campus or service provider. Where *Web* servers speak a computer protocol called HyperText Transport Protocol (HTTP), mail servers speak a computer protocol called Simple Mail Transport Protocol (SMTP). Another analogy for you: the server is like your mailbox. The mailbox is where mail addressed to you is stored until you pick it up. You use your mail client to get your mail from your mailbox.

E-mail links are built within many *Web* pages and allow you to send directed correspondence to other participants through the Internet. Although *Netscape* allows you to send e-mail to others, it doesn't allow you to receive e-mail directly. You can configure the browser to receive mail from a server machine that acts as a mailbox for you, and you can configure it through the *Servers* folder of the *Mail and News Preferences* . . . submenu. However, this will likely involve the cooperation and assistance of a friendly campus computer person so we'll leave the details to them. There are other pieces of software that allow you to receive e-mail. *Eudora* is one of these pieces of software; you may have heard of others. As with *Netscape, Eudora* has a free version, and it is available for both Macintosh and Windows. Manuals that describe its use are common and easily available over the Internet. Some commercial browsers come with the ability to both send and receive e-mail but that may cost a little more money.

If you follow this URL you'll end up on the *QualComm* homepage where you can download either the free version of *Eudora* or get information on the more powerful commercial version. You can also download a copy of the basic user manual.

http://www.qualcomm.com/quest/

The following URLs are *Web* based *Eudora* manuals. Remember to save a bookmark.

http://www.cdtl.umn.edu/eudora_http/contents.html
http://www.netspot.unisa.edu.au/eudora/contents.html

Access to an e-mail server is easily available. If you are at a campus that has provided you with Internet access, you should also have the ability to apply for an e-mail account through your campus computer administration. If your school does not have an e-mail server for students, you still have the option of applying for an e-mail account through an independent service provider like CompuServe or America Online. In fact, if you've already gone through a service provider for access to the Internet, you probably already have e-mail capabilities. There are two things that you'll need to know to properly configure your browser for sending e-mail: (1) your e-mail address and (2) the name of your mail server. You can enter your e-mail information through the *Preferences Mail and News . . .* submenu under *Options*. Once you open the preference dialog window, you should select the *Identity* folder to set up your personal e-mail information for the *Servers* folder (Figure 13) to identify the computer that will act as your mailer. Once you've entered the correct information and restarted the browser program, you should have the ability to send e-mail. Think about it! It means saving postage and long distance phone calls.

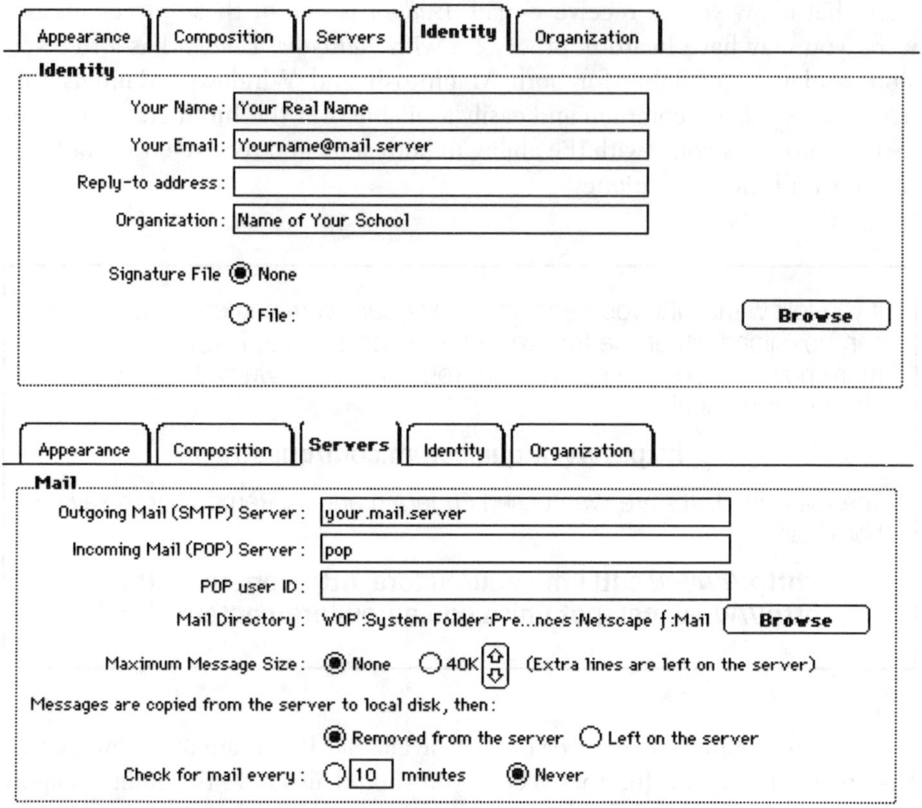

Figure 13. The information about your particular mail server and e-mail address must be entered before you have the ability to send e-mail to others through *Netscape*.

E-mail addresses typically take a very distinctive format. Here is the format of a typical e-mail address: NAME@HOST.DOMAIN. It is not necessary to have a full name for the NAME part of the address, and in fact, some addresses use only numbers to represent an individual. The @ symbol always follows the individual's name and then the name of the mail server computer (HOST). The domain in the e-mail format, just like the domain of the URL format, is used to denote the affiliation of the user. Notice that there are no spaces anywhere in an e-mail address.

Here are examples of typical e-mail addresses. There are four basic components to a typical e-mail address.

nbenokraitis@ubmail.ubalt.edu
abeno@vt.edu

Here are the four components:

individual	nbenokraitis	abeno
mail server	ubmail	(included in location)*
location	ubalt (University of Baltimore)	vt (Virginia Tech)
domain	edu	edu

* Note: Some e-mail addresses might not have a mail server. Some servers can automatically sort what is and what isn't e-mail.

Drop us a brief note if you have some suggestions for making this manual better. (E-mail addresses are not case sensitive.)

Newsgroups

A second feature incorporated by many browsers is the ability to exchange ideas over something called Netnews or Newsgroups. A newsgroup is a group of people that connect to and participate in a specialized discussion. These groups are open forums, and all are welcome to contribute in the interchange. Some are moderated by an individual or individuals who will post items for discussion and referee the electronic brawls that might ensue. Others are free-form and function much more like a street fight. The bottom line with all newsgroups is to have a central place where people can bring to the table new ideas and perspectives. No, not all newsgroups are places for disagreement. Many are very good, with courteous people and polite conversation.

Newsgroups are nearly the opposite of e-mail. Where e-mail is sent and posted for a single person to read, news postings are sent to a common place for all to read and comment. By now you've noticed that I like using analogies. Here is yet another analogy that will help you understand the nature of a newsgroup. If e-mail is like the postal service, newsgroups are like coffee houses on open microphone night.

Okay, so what is the purpose of the newsgroups if people just contribute ideas and comments to a mass discussion on a particular topic? Newsgroups are places where you can ask questions, get ideas, and generally learn about specifics. Select a group that has an interest common to yours or a topic that you are trying to learn something about. You'll find that there are many newsgroups that focus on social science or related issues.

The names of newsgroups are usually descriptive of their discussion topic. There are several major newsgroup categories. The one you'll use most is the SOC group. This group contains discussions about cultural and social issues. Other newsgroups include COMP.SOCIETY for topics specific to computers and social responsibility, SOC.SUPPORT for people coping with depression or family crises, and ALT for alternative topics, which typically encompass serious-minded or controversial social, economic, political, or religious ideas. We've included a list of sociology-related newsgroups in Appendix IV. You'll find some of them interesting and helpful as a supplement to your studies in sociology.

Here is an example of a typical newsgroup URL. Newsgroup names are divided into several descriptive words separated by a period and organized into a hierarchy. Notice that newsgroup URLs don't use the double slash (//).

news:alt.sci.sociology

Here are the three components:

protocol	news:
top category	alt
subcategory	sci
subcategory	sociology

To configure your browser to connect to a newsgroup, you will need the name of the server computer that handles newsgroups. Figure 14 illustrates the preference dialog where you will need to enter your news server name. This may or may not be the same computer that handles your e-mail and *Web* services. News servers use yet another protocol beyond HTTP and SMTP. News servers use a protocol called NetNews Transfer Protocol or NNTP.

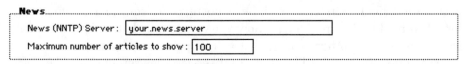

Figure 14. With *Netscape*, the dialog window where you will enter the name of your news server can be found in the *Mail and News Preference* submenu under the *Options* menu.

Once you have an e-mail address, the name of your mail server (SMTP server), and the name of your news server, you're set. If you are using *Netscape*, you can configure your browser by selecting *Preferences* from the *Option* menu. Within the preference window that appears, you must select *Mail and News* from the pull-down option box and then enter your information as illustrated in Figures 13 and 14. If you do not have *Netscape* there are many free news readers for many computer platforms. Personally, even though I have *Netscape*, I use other programs specifically for news reading: *WinVN* or even *Clear Agent* will work great.

The only way to really understand what newsgroups are like is to try them. Here are a couple of newsgroups that will get you started. Connect to one of interest and read some of the postings. You can find a larger list in Appendix IV. For your first time, you should just read the postings and follow some of the conversations. Connections or threads develop between postings as people add comments to earlier postings. As you become familiar with the topic of discussion you might post a comment yourself.

news:soc.rights.human
news:soc.men
news:soc.women

To get the real flavor of a newsgroup you need to spend more than just a couple of minutes viewing one. Choose a newsgroup of interest. Within that newsgroup select a topic that is being discussed and follow it for a week. As a discussion grows, you'll notice that many people will jump in to participate.

Section 3.3
There's no place like home.

There *is* no place like home. You may or may not have found some place on the *Web* that you are willing to call home, but if you haven't found one, then hopefully you'll be able to use the following description to create one for yourself. It is not as simple as browsing the *Web* but it's not very hard either. If your campus has a *Web* server, then it may have a place for student homepages. Ask around to see if you are allowed to keep a homepage there. If you can't get access through your campus, you still have other options. Some of the pages that you view on your browser reside on a *Web* server, but you can also create a file on your home computer or even on a floppy disk that will act as a homepage for you. Admittedly, in order for your homepage to be on the Internet, you'd need access to a *Web* server; but it's not necessary for the basics that I'll describe here. Another option is to use a private service provider to gain access to the Internet. Some service providers rent space to keep homepages on their server. One of the latest things is the idea of the Internet Coffee House. There are several that have just opened. They'll serve up great coffee and provide you with access to the *Web*. Some have even gone as far as renting space for homepages. Search one out.

Homepages

Homepage this and homepage that. What good is a homepage? You will find other uses but here are a couple of reasons I keep a homepage. I use a homepage to organize my important and frequently accessed links and bookmarks to the Internet. Most importantly, these are links and bookmarks to sociology resources all over the world. It's better than a library card. I also keep links to on-line magazines, the weather at my favorite camping spots, movie, music, and book reviews, the current news reports, my school's homepage, my friends' pages, the manuals for my e-mail and *Web* clients, and my favorite search engines and directories. I've even seen students create hyperlink pages that they gave to their instructors as homework assignments. Imagine turning in an assignment where your instructor could use a *Web* browser to link to your references and resources on the Internet.

Now, where is yours? Actually, I've already made one for you. All you have to do is add the stuff about yourself and the links that you think are interesting. Once you've done that, it's all downhill. If you look at Appendix V, you'll see that there is a lot of gibberish that may or may not look like computer programming to you. This is the homepage that I've written for you, and it's written in HTML. HTML is a language that *Web* browsers use to read hypertext documents. It stands for HyperText Markup Language. It's a very simple computer language. In fact, it's so simple that it ranks closer to slang than language. Although this homepage in its present state is quite generic, you'll have plenty of opportunity at the end-of-chapter exercise to liven it up. I don't want you to do anything with it yet. I just want you to see what HTML looks like. We have many basics to discuss before you'll do anything reasonable with it.

Just to give you some ideas of what homepages are like, you can use the following URLs to see what others have done. Some of these may appeal to you while others may be excessive. Homepage design is a personal choice.

The People Page
   http://www.peoplepage.com/

Useless Pages
   http://www.chaco.com/useless/

Cool Page
   http://pages.prodigy.com/CoolPage/indexlowgraphics.html

Best of the Net
   http://gnn.com/gnn/wic/botn/index.html

HTML

The gibberish that you saw on the template homepage in Appendix V is really pretty easy to understand. There are only a couple of things that you need to remember in order to read HTML. If you ignore the HTML gibberish that you don't quite understand, you'll see that the rest of the document makes sense. You can do this by alternately viewing your homepage file through your browser and then through your word processor. You don't need a fancy program to write HTML, just a word processor and an understanding of the code. Now look at the page with the gibberish. Notice that the HTML gibberish typically, but not always, comes in sets of two. At the very top you'll see a tag like this: <HTML>. A *tag* is an element of HTML code. It is added to the page to emphasize the text that will appear on the viewed *Web* page. Tags always have a angle bracket (<) at the beginning and an opposite angle bracket (>) at the end. Here are a couple of examples: <BODY>, <HEAD>, and <TITLE>. The other part of each tag set has a forward slash (/) preceding the word. Here are the other members of the tag pairs: </BODY>, </HEAD>, and </TITLE>. Tags, when used in sets or pairs, surround a section of text and define the beginning and end of an HTML section. Yes, it is possible to use tags incorrectly, just as it is possible to use English incorrectly. What follows is an example of a properly coded HTML page.

> **<HTML>**
>   **<HEAD>**
>   This is where a description and purpose of the page is written. The material that is here is not intended to be viewed on the browser. It is only used to document the intent of the page.
>   **</HEAD>**
>   **<BODY>**
>   This is where the material that is to be viewed through the browser will be written.
>   **</BODY>**
> **</HTML>**

All properly coded HTML documents are coded with this basic format. Notice the beginning and ending member of each tag pair. Although tags usually operate in pairs, some are used as solitary tags. Here are important examples of solitary tags that you should be aware of because they appear in your generic homepage. When you want to separate sections of text with two spaces you might use the paragraph tag, <P>. Two-line break tags, <BR>, will also do the same thing. If you wanted the browser to make a horizontal line across the viewed page, then you would use a horizontal line tag, <HR>. If you're paying attention to the tags, you'll notice that the tag names are abbreviations of what

33

they do. Remember, you don't really have to absorb all this language now. I made a link on your homepage that jumps you to several HTML resources.

If you really want to jump into this HTML thing, then here are several more resources that will help you go further. I have tried to find the resources that will be most beneficial to beginners.

Webreference
   http://www.webreference.com/

Homepage Construction Kit
   http://nearnet.gnn.com/gnn/netizens/construction.html

The Web Workshop
   http://socrates.math.ohio-state.edu/htmlguide/htmltutor.html

Writing HTML
   http://www.mcli.dist.maricopa.edu/tut/

Many other people have already written cool homepages and you could use theirs for a template if you don't like the one I wrote. One of the best things about writing HTML is that you really don't have to write it yourself. *Netscape* and many of the other browsers provide a great tool. If you select the *Source . . .* sub-menu under the *View* menu at the top of your screen, the actual HTML code of the page you are viewing will be displayed for you. All you have to do is find the interesting things that others have done and copy the code and modify them to meet your personality.

Hyperlinks

One very important element in HTML is the code for hyperlinks (jumping points within *Web* pages). You know most of what you need to know to create hyperlinks. The HTML tag for a hyperlink is called an anchor and it uses the tag pair <A> and </A>. There are two main components to an anchor tag. The first element is the URL and the second is the word (or words) to be set as a hyperlink. Here is an example of an anchor tag.

```
<A HREF="URL">
  Word
</A>
```

This is a little more that the <A> and </A> that I described earlier but it's still not that hard. I'll dismantle it for you and you can see how it works. The first line of the example above begins the code for an anchor. Notice again the <A>, but also notice that there is a lot more garbage thrown in between the A and the last angle bracket. You should also notice that this garbage is a URL. This URL tells the browser the location of the requested document. The second line is the text as it will appear on the HTML page (the button, so to speak). Because it will be a hypertext link, it will appear as a colored link to your browser. The anchor tag set is completed with the ending anchor tag, </A>. As it operates on an actual *Web* page, if the user selects the hypertext link, then the user will be sent the document specified by the URL.

Now for an exercise. Use your word processor and type in the basic page elements that I gave to you earlier (<HTML> and </HTML>). Within the body of the page I want you to type in an anchor tag set using a real URL. Use one or both of the examples provided below. Once you have this page, save it with the name TEST.HTML and view it with your browser.

A Beginners Guide to HTML
http://www.ncsa.uiuc.edu/General/Internet/WWW/
HTMLPrimer.html

How to Publish On The *Web*
http://www.thegiim.org/

See step #2 in the section below for help in finding and displaying this file. Once you've got this page up and running on your browser, try the hyperlink. Does it work? You should notice that these URLs will take you to resources that will tell you more about *Web* publishing.

Home

So, you have a homepage. Where do you put it to make it work? Well, this depends on whether you will have access to a *Web* server or not. I'll assume that you don't and give you some instructions that will still help you use it to your advantage. Once you've completed your homepage, you'll have a file on either your hard drive or a floppy disk. The advantage of having your homepage on floppy disk is that you'll have a portable homepage that you can use on any computer. I'll give you a five-step procedure for finding and setting your default homepage to the one you've created.

1. *After* you finished the end-of-chapter exercise, you should copy your intended homepage to either a floppy disk or your hard drive.
2. With *Netscape* you should notice that there is a command under the *File* menu called *Open File . . ..* If you initiate this command, you'll get a dialog window where you can designate the file you wish to open. The trick to this is that this file isn't on a server. Select the HTML file from either your floppy drive or hard drive and press the Return key on your keyboard. Because your file is written in HTML your browser will open up and display it for you.
3. If it isn't set already, change your Options setting so that you can view the URLs of the pages that display on your browser. When this is set properly, you'll notice that your file's URL is listed something like this: **file:/// . . . ./file.html**. Notice that the protocol is not HTTP and that you may have more than two slashes.
4. Record this URL on a piece of paper so that you can refer to it in the next step. I would ask you to remember it and copy it to step 5 but every little slash and colon is important. So, this will save you from a possible SNAFU (Situation Normal. All Fouled Up). I learned this from a friend in the Army.
5. If you remember from earlier in this chapter, I described how you can change the homepage designation for your browser. Go back to this section and use the description to open the General Preferences section of the Options menu. Open the folder for *Appearance* reference and enter the URL that you wrote down from step 4 into the homepage entry window.

Now that you've performed these steps, your browser should automatically jump you onto your homepage when you select the Home button from the toolbar. Give it a try. The procedures that you've just performed have allowed your browser to memorize the location of your homepage file. If you move it or erase it, then you'll have to do this all over again. Builds character—right?

Run Wild

There are many more tags than I have the space to describe here or, for that matter, that you probably want to know right now. They are not hard to learn, and in fact, there are places on the *Web* that offer on-line tutorials on HTML design. Once you have your homepage operational, you'll see that I included links to some of these places for you. As you learn more about the Internet, the *Web*, and HTML, you'll discover ways to add pictures to your pages. Later you'll even begin adding sounds and maybe a video clip or two. We are at the beginning of a new way of learning and communicating.

The tools available to you at this moment are only a hint of what will be available to you in a year. For example, there are a number of companies developing software that allow you to create "rich *Web* documents without programming." Check out HTML Pro, Adobe PageMill or SiteMill, InContext Spider, or Microsoft Internet Assistant for Word. If I could give you one bit of advice on your journeys through this new world, this *World Wide Web*, it would be to *watch*, *look*, and *listen* to your world.

Activity
Make yourself at home!

The activity of the day is to make your own homepage with bookmarks. One of the greatest problems that I have, as a teacher and administrator of a student network, is the gradual and insidious buildup of cluttersome bookmarks. The situation is obvious: each student changes the browsers on the computers in my classroom to meet his or her personal needs. I never know what to expect when I need to teach a class or use a browser. Students, with much less experience, are confused and disoriented. I have, to some extent, come up with a solution.

The gibberish that you will see in Appendix V is my solution. It is a template for a student homepage to be kept on a floppy disk. The added value in this is that you can also use this generic homepage as a portable resource disk on most networked computers. Still the only drawback is that you can't jump between Macintosh and Windows with this arrangement. But then, I'll leave that up to the computer giants.

You should know a couple of conventions so that you will understand what you need to do. I have used a *large italic font* to represent the text that you are to replace with your information. HTML tags are represented in a <SMALLER FONT, ALL IN UPPER-CASE AND WITH ANGLE BRACKETS>. Text that is not an HTML tag and *does not* need to be changed is in a regular size and font.

To create a homepage on a floppy disk simply use any word processor to type the information onto a floppy disk. Give the file a name with the suffix html (HOMENAME.HTML). Once this is done, you should follow the instructions in section 3.3 to adapt it to your liking. Remember to show some style and personality!

Glossary
It's all Greek to me

Archie   This is a search tool used to find resources that are stored on Internet-based FTP servers. Archie is short for Archive because it performs an archive search for resources. (see FTP and Server)

AVI   This stands for Audio/Video Interleaved. It is a Microsoft Corporation format for encoding video and audio for digital transmission.

Background   This refers to an image or color that is present in the background of a viewed *Web* document. Complex images are becoming very popular as backgrounds but require a great deal more time to download. The color of default background can be set for most *Web* browsers.

Bookmark   This refers to a list of URLs saved within a browser. The user can edit and modify the bookmark list to add and delete URLs as the user's interests change. Bookmark is a term used by *Netscape* to refer to the user's list of URLs while 'Hotlist' is used by *Mosaic* to refer to the same list. (see Hotlist, *Mosaic*, and URL)

Browser   This is a software program that is used to view and browse information on the Internet. Browsers are also referred to as clients. (see Client)

Bulletin Board Service   This is an electronic bulletin board. It is sometimes referred to as a BBS. Information on a BBS is posted to a computer where many can dial in and read it and/or comment on it. BBS's may or may not be connected to the Internet. Some are accessible by modem dial-in only.

Cache   This refers to a section of memory that is set aside to store information that is commonly used by the computer or an active piece of software. Most browsers will create a cache to commonly accessed images. An example might be the images that are common to the user's homepage. Retrieving images from the cache is much quicker than downloading the images from the original source each time they are required.

Clickable image (Clickable map)   This refers to an interface used in *Web* documents that allow the user to click or select different areas of an image and receive different responses. Clickable images are becoming very common as a way of offering a user many different selections within a common visual format.

Client   This is a software program used to view information from remote computers. Clients function in a Client-Server information exchange model. This term may also be loosely applied to the computer that is used to request information from the server. (see Server)

Compressed file   This refers to a file or document that has been compacted to save memory space so that it can be easily and quickly transferred through the Internet.

Download   This is the process of transferring a file, document, or program from a remote computer to a local computer. (see Upload)

E-mail   This is the short name for electronic mail. E-mail is sent electronically from one person to another. Some companies have e-mail systems that are not part of the Internet. E-mail can also be sent to one person or to many different people. I sometimes refer to this as JunkE-mail. You form your own opinions.

FAQ   This stands for Frequently Asked Questions. A FAQ is a file or document where a moderator or administrator will post commonly asked questions and their answers. Although it is very easy to communicate across the Internet, if you have a question, you should check for the answer in a FAQ first.

Forms   This refers to an interface element used within *Web* documents to allow user to send information back to a *Web* server. With a forms interface, the user is requested to type responses within entry windows to be returned to the server for processing. Forms rely on a server computer to process the submittals. They are becoming more common as browser and server software improve.

FTP   This stands for File Transfer Protocol. It is a procedure used to transfer large files and programs from one computer to another. Access to the computer to transfer files may or may not require a password. Some FTP servers are set up to allow public access by anonymous log-on. This process is referred to as *Anonymous FTP*.

GIF   This stands for Graphics Interchange Format. It is a format created by CompuServe to allow electronic transfer of digital images. GIF files are a common and much used format and can be viewed by both Mac and Windows users.

Gopher   A format structure and resource for providing information on the Internet. It was created at the University of Minnesota.

GUI   An acronym for Graphical User Interface. It is a combination of the appearance and the method of interacting with a computer. A GUI requires the use of a mouse to select commands on an icon-based monitor screen. Macintosh and Windows operating systems are typical GUI examples.

Homepage   In its specific sense, this refers to a *Web* document that a browser loads as its central navigational point to browse the Internet. It may also be used to refer to as *Web* page describing an individual. In the most general sense, it is used to refer to any *Web* document.

Hotlist   This is a list of URL's saved within the *Mosaic Web* browser. This same list is referred to as a Bookmark within the *Netscape Web* browser.

HTML   An abbreviation for HyperText Markup Language, the common language used to write documents that appear on the *World Wide Web*.

HTTP   An abbreviation for HyperText Transport Protocol, the common protocol used to communicate between *World Wide Web* servers.

Hypertext   This refers to text elements within a document that have an embedded connection to another item. *Web* documents use hypertext links to access documents, images, sounds, and video files from the Internet. The term hyperlink is a general term that applies to elements on *Web* pages other than text.

Inline image   This refers to images that are viewed along with text on *Web* documents. All inline images are in the GIF format. JPEG format is the other common image format for *Web* documents, but an external viewer is typically required to view them.

JPEG   This stands for Joint Photographic Experts Group. It is also commonly used to refer to a format used to transfer digital images.

Jughead   This is a service for performing searches on the Internet. (see Archie and Veronica)

Mosaic   This is the name of the browser that was created at the National Center for Supercomputing Applications. It was the first *Web* browser to have a consistent interface for the Macintosh, Windows, and UNIX environments. The success of this browser is really responsible for the expansion of the *Web*.

MPEG   This stands for Motion Picture Experts Group. It is also a format used to make, view, and transfer both digital audio and digital video files.

Newsgroup   This the name for the discussion groups that can be on the Usenet. Not all newsgroups are accessible through the Internet. Some are accessible only through a modem connection.

QuickTime   This is a format used by Apple Computer to make, view, edit, and send digital audio and video.

Server   This is a software program used to provide, or serve, information to remote computers. Servers function in a Client-Server information exchange model. This term may also be loosely applied to the computer that is used to serve the information. (see Client)

Table   This refers to a specific formatting element found in HTML pages. Tables are used on HTML documents to visually organize information.

Telnet   This is the process of remotely connecting and using a computer at a distant location.

Upload   This is the process of moving or transferring a document, file, or program from one computer to another computer.

URL   This is an abbreviation for Universal Resource Locator. In its basic sense it is an address used by people on the Internet to locate documents. URLs take a common format that describe the protocol for information transfer, the host computer address, path to the desired file, and the name of the file requested.

Usenet   This is a world-wide system of discussion groups, also called news-groups. There are many thousands of newsgroups, but only a percentage are accessible from the Internet.

Veronica   Believe it or not, this is an acronym. It stands for Very Easy Rodent Oriented Net-wide Index to Computerized Archives. This is a database of menu names from a large number of Gopher servers. It is a quick and easy way to search Gopher resources for information by keyword. It was developed at the University of Nevada.

WAIS   This stands for Wide Area Information Servers. This is a software package that allows the searching of large indexes of information from the Internet.

WAV   This stands for Waveform sound format. It is a Microsoft Corporation format for encoding sound files.

Web (WWW)   This stands for the *World Wide Web*. When loosely applied, this term refers to the Internet and all of its associated incarnations, such as Gopher, FTP, HTTP, etc. More specifically, this term refers to a subset of the servers on the Internet that use HTTP to transfer hyperlinked document in a page-like format.

Appendix I
What's under the hood?

Here is a computer question to get your mind working. What is the difference between a Corvette and a Cavalier? Okay, it's a stupid question, but think about it. The difference is a couple thousand dollars. Everything else is just fluff, mileage, and auto insurance. But if we break this down to our basic needs (if we really need a ride), both cars are the same. The same goes for computers and networks. The simple no-gloss stuff will get you by while saving you money; and the high-gloss stuff will transform your cash into dash and make your Internet browsing a little more enjoyable. Many of you have computers on your campus that are set up to allow Internet access. In case you don't, I'll list the *minimum* systems, connections, and services that you'll need to enter the Internet, but you'll have to decide how shiny your system needs to be.

The Computer
Now watch how you approach this issue if you ask for advice on which computer to buy. Opinions are known to run a little hot with some people when they begin to argue the differences between Macintosh and PC-compatible systems. Proponents from both camps can easily get out of hand. If they begin to foam at the mouth, then you know you're in for a real adventure. The best advice that I can give to you is test them both at a computer store. Choose the one that you can pay for and are most comfortable using. After all, it won't do you any good if you don't enjoy using it or if it gets repossessed halfway through the semester.

These are the minimum system items that you'll need:

Macintosh
- 68020
- System 7.0
- 256 color monitor
- 8 MB of RAM
- 4 MB of free disk space for browser software

PC-Compatible
- Intel 386sx
- Windows 3.1
- VGA monitor
- 8 MB of RAM
- 4 MB of free disk space for browser software

The Internet Connection

Your campus may already be using the Internet as a teaching and learning tool. If the equipment is set up, then it should have Internet, or more specifically *Web* access ready to go. If not, there are many resources that can help you set up a connection from home.

Some campuses, although lacking a walk-in lab, have made arrangements for students to dial into the campus computer system and, hopefully, the Internet. If this is the case, then search out the campus computer hack and ask for help.

Another option for accessing the Internet is to subscribe to a company such as America Online, CompuServe, Delphi, Prodigy, or Microsoft. Many other companies, such as AT&T, Bell Atlantic, and MCI, are also in business to sell you access to the Internet and you should consider them in addition to these five. Some of these on line service providers advertise the availability of access. However, you are required to use their software and it may not have all of the options that you might want. As always, it is a buyer's market and you should shop around and test drive everything before you buy.

When it comes to buying modems, I suggest you buy something as fast as possible, but not a modem of less than 14,400 bits per second (bps). A bps is a measure of the speed with which the modem transfers data. The higher the number, usually the faster the transfer rate. With a typical 14.4K baud modem you can expect that it will take a few seconds to transfer a typical *Web* page, but this will vary depending on the complexity of the page. There are a couple of other things that come into play, but in general, a higher number means a faster modem.

The Browser Software

If everything has fallen into place, you should now have access to a computer with muscle and a gateway to the Internet, either through your school or an Internet service provider. But you're missing one very important piece, the *Web* client software. A more descriptive name for this software is *browser*, as that is what most people do with it. It is used to browse or wander, usually purposefully but sometimes aimlessly, through the Internet.

There are many *Web* browsers on the market and in the space of time that it's taken me to write this manual I would not doubt that several more have entered the race to capture your dollar. The mother of all browsers is NCSA's *Mosaic*, now in version 2.00, but there have been many others spawned from it. Although you might have contrasting opinions when you've tried a couple, I prefer Netscape Communication's *Netscape Navigator* (version 2.0 as I write this), and therefore, I've chosen to use it to illustrate this manual. All browsers have advantages and disadvantages. Although I prefer *Netscape* as my vehicle for Internet travel, you may find *Mosaic* or *Microsoft Internet Explorer* or another to be more to your liking. I have included a list of many of the available browsers in the Appendix. You should really evaluate them all and choose the one that you're most comfortable with. Browsers are typically very cheap, if not simply free for educational use. *Netscape, Mosaic,* and many of the other browsers are FREE for student use! So, don't be afraid to evaluate them all.

Now, if you have all of these basic elements and they've been put together correctly, you should be ready to surf. The rest of this manual is devoted to guiding you through some of the many strange and wonderful places that will allow you to enjoy the depth and uniqueness of the field of sociology.

Appendix II
Eyeglasses and spyglasses

Web Browsers

AIR Mosaic
SPRY Inc.
Seattle, WA
800-777-9638, ext. 26
206-447-0300
206-447-9008 fax
info26@spry.com

Cello
Cornell Law School Legal Information Institute
Ithaca, NY
lii@fatty.law.cornell.edu

Enhanced NCSA Mosaic
Spyglass Inc.
Naperville, IL
708-505-1010
708-505-4944 fax
info@spyglass.com

Netscape Navigator
Netscape Communications Corp.
Mountain View, CA
800-638-7483
415-254-1900
415-254-2601 fax
info@mcom.com

NCSA Mosaic
National Center for Supercomputing Applications
University of Illinois
Champagne, IL
217-244-3473
orders@ncsa.uiuc.edu

NetCruiser
Netcom On-Line Communications Services Inc.
San Jose, CA
800-501-8649
408-983-5970
408-241-9145 fax
info@netcom.com

InterAp
California Software Inc.
714-675-9906
714-675-3646 fax
support@calsoft.com

Web Explorer
IBM Corp.
Armonk, NY
800-342-6672
800-426-6063 fax

WinTapestry
Frontier Technologies Corp.
Mequon, WI
414-241-4555
414-241-7084 fax
superhighway@frontiertech.com

WinWeb
EINet
Austin TX
800-844-4638
512-338-3897 fax
winWeb@einet.net

Appendix III
A call to order

Internet Providers

America Online
America Online Inc.
8619 Westwood Center Dr.
Vienna, VA 22182-2285
800-827-6364
703-448-8700
aohotline@aol.com

CompuServe
CompuServe Inc.
5000 Arlington Centre Blvd.
Columbus, OH 43220
800-848-8199
614-457-8600
70006,101@compuserve.com

Delphi
Delphi Internet Services Corp.
1030 Massachusetts Ave.
Cambridge, MA 02138
800-695-4005
617-491-3342
617-491-6642 fax
askdelphi@delphi.com

Prodigy
Prodigy Services Co.
445 Hamilton Ave.
White Plains, NY 10601
800-776-3449

If you don't want to use one of these large service providers but would prefer a company that drops the frills and gives you direct access to the Internet, you can locate such service providers at this *Web* address (**http://www. celestin.com/pocia/domestic/d_rega.html**). Just search by the area code for your phone service and you'll get a list of providers that will accept your money to use their service. Remember, also, to check out your public library. Many provide access to the Internet for a nominal annual fee.

Appendix IV
It's news to me

Sociology Newsgroups

Think of this as a starter kit to the Usenet. This is not a complete list and some of the newsgroups will undoubtedly disappear. Additionally, there are many new groups that emerge every month. One of them might even be yours.

The names are very descriptive for the topic of discussion. You will find that some are very interesting and some are not. Subscribe to several of the groups and eavesdrop on their conversations for a while before you jump in. This will give you some experience with the general attitude of the group and prevent some embarrassment on your part. We also suggest that you read the FAQ and any postings directed to new participants to the group.

    alt.culture.internet
    alt.homosexual
    alt.org.earth-first
    alt.religion.islam
    alt.sci.sociology
    alt.society.civil-disob
    alt.society.generation-x
    alt.society.paradigms
    alt.society.revolution
    bit.listserv.sos-data
    comp.society
    comp.society.development
    comp.society.folklore
    rec.bicycles.soc
    soc.college
    soc.college.gradinfo
    soc.couples

soc.culture.african
soc.culture.african.american
soc.culture.arabic
soc.culture.asian.american
soc.culture.canada
soc.culture.indian
soc.feminism
soc.genealogy.misc
soc.culture.irish
soc.culture.italian
soc.culture.japan
soc.culture.usa
soc.genealogy.slavic
soc.net-people
soc.penpals
soc.religion.christian
soc.religion.eastern
soc.singles
soc.support.depression.misc
soc.support.fat-acceptance
soc.support.transgendered
soc.support.youth.gay-lesbian-bi
soc.veterans
soc.history.war.vietnam
soc.history.what-if
soc.college.financial-aid
soc.retirement
soc.culture.baltics
soc.culture.intercultural
talk.abortion
talk.atheism
talk.mideast
talk.philosophy
talk.politics

Appendix V
Stepping Out

Student Homepage Template

```
<HTML>
<HEAD>
        <TITLE>Your Homepage</TITLE>
</HEAD>
</BODY>
<CENTER>
        <H1>Your Name</H1>
        <H2>Your Title, Major, or Philosophy</H2>
        <H3>
        <ADDRESS>
                Your address<BR>
                May<BR>
                Go<BR>
                Here<BR>
                <P>
                Your e-mail address<BR>
        </ADDRESS>
        </H3>
</CENTER>
<HR>
<DL>
        <H2>This Is Your Life:</H2>
        <DD>Just say something about yourself. After you've added
            something to your homepage file compare it to what
            actually shows on your browser. You'll notice that most
            of this gibberish is not visible.
        <P>
```

<DD>*You can have as many paragraphs as you wish. Here's another. Enjoy.*
<P>
</DL>

<DL>

<H2>Important Sociology Resources</H2>
<DD>
<A HREF="http://www.asanet.org/">
Web Resource for the American Sociological Association
</A>
</DL>
<HR>
<DL>

<H2>Handbooks and Manuals</H2>
<DD>
<A HREF="http://www.matisse.net/files/glossary.html">
Glossary of Internet Terms
</A>
<DD>
<A HREF="http://www.cdtl.umn.edu/eudora_http/contents.html">
Eudora Manual
</A>
<DD>
<A HREF="http://home.netscape.com/eng/mozilla/2.0/handbook/">
Netscape Handbook
</A>
</DL>
<HR>
<DL>

<H2>Directories and Search Engines: </H2>
<DD>
<A HREF="http://lycos.cs.cmu.edu/">
Lycos Search Engine
</A>
<DD>
<A HREF="http://www.yahoo.com/">
Yahoo Directory
</A>
</DL>
<HR>

<DL>

<H2>Design and Publish: </H2>
<DD>
<A HREF="http://www.ncsa.uiuc.edu/General/Internet/WWW/HTMLPrimer.html">
A Beginner's Guide to HTML
</A>
<DD>
<A HREF="http://werbach.com/barebones/">

The BareBones Guide to HTML
```
    </A>
  <DD>
    <A HREF="http://www.thegiim.org/">
```
How to Publish On The *Web*
```
    </A>
</DL>
<HR>
<H3>
```
Your Name `<A HREF="mailto:Name@server.edu">`e-mail address`</A>`
```
</H3>

</BODY>
</HTML>
```